ABOUT THE AUTHOR

Ben North lives in London with his wife, too many books and two
brain tumours.

He tweets @inkib and his Instagram handle is inkynorth. His Twitter
account is rarely serious and contains a lot of sarcasm and swearing,
as well as new poetry every now and again. His IG account also
includes the odd bit of illustration and photography.

One of the poems in this collection was shortlisted for the 2018
Bridport Poetry Prize. You'll have to guess which one.

GW00382115

THIRTY-THREE POEMS

SOME OF WHICH ARE ABOUT DEATH

BEN NORTH

For Lana. My true north.

CONTENTS

AN INTRODUCTION

This is how the book you are currently reading came about.

I started writing poetry in the early 90s as a predictably rather intense young man. After a few years I (mostly) stopped for a long time, a period which coincided with me repeatedly not writing several novels.

In 2017 I discovered two poems from around 2010/11, which I had forgotten about. I didn't dislike them, and so I began writing again.

The approach I took was to unromantically bang out quick ideas, often on the commute to work, almost always on my phone. I limited myself to three or four revisions, then sent them to writer friends – whether they wanted them or not – just to mark them as completed so that I could move on to the next idea: a sort of 'fast poetry'.

I was enjoying this way of working, the sense of just getting *anything* written, and at least some of the results. Then, in October of 2017, I discovered that, entirely without my permission, my body had been busy growing an aggressive brain tumour (I have recently acquired another one).

In 2018 I put together a selection of old and new poems (a friend had, fortunately, been able to find copies of some 'lost' early poems) and had it published as a private chapbook to give to family and friends, and, perhaps most importantly, just to hold in my own hands.

To my surprise, a wider group of acquaintances asked if they could buy copies. As the chapbook (*Slow Then Fast*) wasn't a commercial venture, I suggested that they donate to The Brain Tumour Charity and then I would send or give them a copy. This proved to be a fairly successful fundraising effort.

Despite my attention and energy being very limited these days, I have continued to write at a reasonable pace and now have a store of new poems. Many of these are more stylistically and thematically diverse than before. As I was still being asked if it was possible to acquire some sort of collection of my work, I decided to put this slim volume together and make it available to a wider audience. While being heavily influenced by recent events, a range of subjects is represented here, including love, relationships, nature and myth.

Finally, I should make it clear that these poems are not presented chronologically, and some that survived from the original chapbook have been edited or partially rewritten.

B~

Harp

Everyone hates
harmonicas.
Always louder
than you think.

Sandwich metal,
wood and reeds.
Hold it in both
hands and blow.

It upsets some
that so little skill
and such a simple
thing makes music.

Fuck it.
Blow them away.

On Hearing The Cure's 'Plainsong' for the First Time
After a Terminal Cancer Diagnosis

It's
like
the
end
of the
world
made
beautiful
past
bearing.

A
shatter
ed
melody
falling
into
the
infinite
played
by
shadows
with starlight
instruments.

This
sound
gives
me
brief
hope
for a
shining,
clamorous,
spectacular
death.

It
lasts
five
minutes
and
seventeen
seconds.

The Cities of L

Are many and
contain multitudes.

Have a heart you can't help but hear.

Open late and taste incredible.

Never cease to surprise and
are best walked through.

Contradict themselves
delightfully, daily.

Will not be other than
what they are.

Have balconies and bars
which do not close if there is life
still in the night.

Do not care for your itinerary.

Know that art should be in
life as much as life in art.

Are home to cats.

Are beautiful.

Are where I wish to live out all my days.

Some Day Soon I Shall Care Again About

Those four very good reasons you had for
not getting back to me when I needed you to.

Your passionate beliefs about why
some people are problematic.

That cousin of yours who had the same thing and
he ate turmeric every day and now he's better.

If I have offended or confused you.

That problem you are still having with
that one guy at work.

The future of the planet.

Raising my voice in public and it
making people uncomfortable.

Today may not be that day.

Death as a Young Boy

When he was a young boy,
Death was very lonely.

The other children wouldn't
play with him. 'You're creepy,'

they said. 'You can't be a part of our
gang. Go and sit somewhere else.

'And what's with all the black?
Are you some sort of loser Goth?'

As he grew up, Death would
sometimes run into his old

schoolmates in the street, or
down the pub, but still they

didn't want to know him. He
tried to be friendly, but they

weren't having it. 'Go away,
weirdo,' they'd say, waving him

out of the way of the giant TV
with the big match on it. But

as they got older, every now
and again they would call him

over to chat a bit about this
and that, the kids, work, that

ache they had which just got
worse. Then one day he found

to his delight that he was
the most popular guy around.

The Night When Every Star Was Seen

Stinging cold; and
everything glitters
so sharp
if a fingernail tapped it
this scene would ring
clear and clean
on the night when every star was seen.

Reading Hemingway in Costa with
cancer

Don't give a fuck if I oughta
All that shit fades away
When you sit in this
fucking seat

Resignation

It was only shop work,
always has been, always will be.
There were lies on both sides.
From me the stuff about
an interest in business,
enjoying meeting people
and being part of a team.
Well, I'm a loner –
always will be, always have been.
From them, the one about
rewarding loyalty – though
never with money – and the
stuff about shop-floor staff
having always been the glue
that held the company
together, and saw them through.
I may have been a cynic
but I was a young cynic
so I half bought it.
At least I was only half disappointed
when it all turned out to be shit.
Oh, and by the way
didn't they use to make horses into glue?
Sad old dead horses,
drudges worn down to death
that never got to run
around thrilling green courses.

Make Only Essential Journeys

To the bar where you are
the first customer of the day.

To a bookshop to find a book
that hasn't yet been written.

From the brightness of the train station
steps to the dank grandeur of the palazzo.

From the one to the four to the five.

To meet an old friend you have
taken for granted and kiss them.

From the Shire to Mount Doom,
sans giant eagles.

From swirling electric dust to
blacker than black atomic rust.
From an end to a beginning.

On Early Waking in Late Summer

...snap back blind, open window.
Clear lungs and eyes clouded with sleep,
breathing, rubbing away.
Silent, not silenced. It is enough
to gaze
blink
sniff
unruly garden. Wet.

Wishing to feel this way
for every heartbeat remaining
I turn inside to face the day.

This Is a Lie

I find no poetry in the strange.
There is no romance for me
in foreign lands and crepuscular ruins.
No exotic face has ever caught my breath
like the careworn smile of my neighbour.
I find no savour
on precise plates of luxury.
I wish only for love and a simple life,
love and a simple life.

Advice

Be a good boy, take the medicine and take it easy.

I like the Eagles – for my
many sins – but an
open-top Cali cruise
is firmly in my bucket bin
and I'm not a boy I'm
a man in a hurry.

See it's only numbers to
you but it's a cold
fire to me 'just wait and
see' has no meaning.

Hurry, hurry up
I'm a man in a hurry
and if you can't
keep up tough
fucking luck.

Come on, come on
time is now give
me what I want
I can't wait around
for you to grow
yourselves up.

Jackdaws on the Terrace at Pembroke Lodge

Hello, little grey eye.
Riding updrafts from the
river valley, snapping out
black wings to spiral over
the handsome white roof of
the lodge where we married,
drank and danced, and
wished those who hadn't
made it this far, had.

But this place is yours much
more than ours. Your endeavours
so serious – the stealing of cake,
the claiming of insects and berries.
Your waddle cheers me no end.
The quick little legs taking you
about your business brook no denial,
and as my smiles are sincere, I hide them.

We haven't returned till now for nearly three years.
I try every day to show you how much I love you.

I Am Not the Poem You Think I Am

I am not the poem you think I am.
I do not encapsulate hope
like the beads of black ink
beneath the skin of my soft right bicep.

I am not flirting with the liminal
for the sake of hard-won insight
into the human condition or the heart of the heart's bloody matter.

I am not trying to move you
but to disappoint with recognition
that we crave these useless things and that cant is universal.

I am a confession of weakness,
a splashing in the shallows of disappointment and the dread
of experience abbreviated.

I am wrong.
Read me as you will.
I am yours now.

The King of Cornwall

Driving down the lanes,
searching for a thing of beauty,
a pasty or some pirate booty,
there's just one man you need to know,
one number you should call.
Me. The King of bloody Cornwall.

I'm the man you need.
Prince of everything
you tourists admire,
potentate of cats
with three legs,
lord of two-headed chickens,
the only one round here
with a full set of thumbs
whose sister
doubles as his mum.

I've said it before looks like I'll say it again.
No. Clue. You.

Tried to make it understood
in rhythm and rhyme.
But. You. No. Clue.

The patient patient waiting
to be asked – a clue?
Not. To. You.

So now, here it is,
plain as plain can be,
you should have been asking me how it is,
what it's like, every second, of every day,
facing my *inevitable* doom.

And shut the fuck up
with *how are you?*

Tiny Fucking Shoes

Little fucking shoes
on normal-sized men.
What a thing.

The uniform
of the half-clever
cunt.
A polo shirt
from Pretty
Green, a tanned
grinning mug,
skinny jeans
and those
little fucking
shoes.

He's the
Tinder King,
a *Bantasaurus
rex*, he loves
a cheeky Nando's
and cheeky
pint or ten
and by then
you'll either
be his brother
or his new best
friend.

What a relief to know you're neither.

I Am King

And will be treated as such.

I was crowned with saw and scalpel.
Now all shall do my bidding
so long as I am enthroned.

I am high priest, lawgiver,
my word runs as writ.
If I wish it, it happens.

Why do you negotiate?
I scratch at my laurel wreath,
hearing 'can't' and 'shouldn't'.

These words.
Mean nothing.
In this grove.

When the time comes
the new King will come
and kill me.

Pagan

Hear this now. *I am no Christian.*

To all those I care not
who ever at all for
did me harm your hand-
knowing or me-down
unknowing. guilt.

I say clearly. *In this I am pagan.*

I have no Your apologies
time to waste mean nothing.
on motivation, Reparation
mitigation must be by
or excuse. blood or gold

Speak not to me. *My time is brief.*

Of cause As I have
and effect. made clear.
The world Stop talking.
is surface It serves
not depth. no use.

A Cornish Holiday

We holiday,
you holiday.
They used to
make us pray
on holy days.

But we'd get
gone from
chapel quickly
as the minister
would allow.

Preachers
be damned.
Those were our
days, days away
from labour.

Days of idle talk,
walking out to
coves and cliffs
unseen, by God
or family.

Days for holy
things like the
undressing
of bodies
in need.

Drinking
beer until we
are on our
knees in
prayer again.

Now we eat fresh
fish and chips,
and ice cream,
'the best pasties
in town'.

Drink good gin,
laugh long
enough for the
tide to go out
and come back in.

Walk it off
on cliff-path
rambles. Swim
in the Hildon-
clear Atlantic.

As Is

As lip is to ear,
so far is to near.

As slip is to cup,
so ewe is to tup.

As knowledge to fact,
so talking to tact.

As promise to present,
so lord is to peasant.

As life is to death,
so warp is to weft.

As lover to loved,
so glover to gloved.

As weight is to heft,
so grace is to deft.

As book is to knowledge,
so farm is to forage.

As own is to theft,
so right is to left.

As house is to home,
so dirt is to loam.

No rest, no remorse,
a rider, no horse.

The close, the insistent,
the desperate, persistent.

We learn, we forget,
and all end up dead.

See Him; He Has a New Fear

See, he fears the treacherous chair.

See, he fears the shaking fork, the spoiled clean shirt.

See, he fears the cold kitchen floor, the refrigerator door, the whoops and moans, the jerking electrical bends.

See, he fears to be left alone.

Sometimes as a child again he fears the dark.

Why fear death, he said, what fear is there to be had in nothingness?

See him; he has a new fear.

Orion

Orion
at the kitchen door
smoking my cigarette of choice
(hand rolled, liquorice paper, menthol filter, if you must).

Thinking about wells and boxes,
about climbing out from rising water.
Thinking about the high night sky.

My old friend Orion.
With his handsome belt and sword.

Hanging above me,
uncaring and comforting.

January, 8am

All wrapped up
in cares and ourselves.
In scarves given by lovers
and fear handed down
the generations.

The smell of bowels
made bad by years of painful
rising before dawn.
The shake of hands palsied
by office anxieties
learned in classrooms at the
whim of bullies and failures
turned teacher.

What lesson does a failure
teach except bitterness and
longing for the day they
hold the whip?

Dick

Once he was asked
if he was famous at
the bus stops outside
Finsbury Park Station.

A woman with a wobbly air of polyaddiction and breakdown gently
ambushed him with her question.

He paused to deny it slightly, laughing as if to say, 'Little me?
Well, no, but thanks for being so lovely as to recognise that I could be.'

He was that sort of dick.

He probably still is.

My Father's Son

He was a big blond man
my dad. Easy to laugh,
easy to smile.

He smoked his way
to a collection of
beautiful soft cigarette packets
saved from trips abroad,
iconic designs
from an age of
triumphant inhaling.

Later he moved to
little tins of ten Café Crème
after-dinner cigarillos, which he drew down like Camels.

He took a good
photograph,
painted butterflies
and flowers well,
loved single malts
and quality blends,
and my mother very much.

Once, frustrated by
some teenage twist from me,
he banged the breakfast table
and briefly raised his voice.
He was in tears half
a moment later.

I had become strange
to him, pained in my skin,
unhappy in the world.

A tumour came for him at forty-five.
Not the lungs, but the brain.

One night I found him in our armchair:
gasping
moaning
jerking
caught up
in what
was once
called
a fit.

Ten months later I raised
a glass to the sky for him.

Early on, from his hospital bed
he lied, told me everything
would be all right.

But it really wasn't.

And now at last, in this at least,
I have become my father's son.

Terminus

At the
terminal
we terminate.

There is no
connection
here. No
flight,
no
train, no
shuttle bus
to save
us from
tarmac rain.

We will
not walk
up motorised
staircases,
be greeted
by smiles
and
a line
of backs
putting
brightly coloured
backpacks
in overhead
lockers
already half full
of coats
and plastic bags
stapled
shut.

There will
be no
wait
for take-off,
no worries
about
screaming babies
in the seat
behind.

No safety
briefing
dance,
no tax-free
shopping
catalogue.

Trackless

How is the air?
The air is sweet,
though there is
a metallic morning tang to it
like the memory
of a future knife
drawn gently across
the tongue.

How far can you see?
Not far, but further than before.

Are there landmarks?
Of sorts. Grey waystones half
cushioned with mossy green
begin just feet away
and run down the incline.
Though soon they are few
and far between and
it is hard to discern
these travellers' friends
from mere stony
outcrops.

There is a valley too
a way below.
A shallow stream runs through it.
Though I cannot
see its source
or destination,
I believe it must start with
a spring and end with a sea.

Could you follow it down?
Perhaps.
But what other paths may
lie hidden over these slopes'
soft horizons?

And when high clouds move
across William's sun
it throws chiaroscuro
camouflage
across the plains
beyond these dales and
diversions, hiding the tiny
signs of habitation I had
thought I might
navigate by.

Soon I must leave
this place of beauty.
This vantage point with no
advantage.

A Sailor Song

I want the sea
and no one but thee.

I want some peace
and a dog twixt my knees.

I want the wind
to be mistress to me.

To sail past the stones
and bring my catch home.

Nuada of the Silver Arm

This morning the day
seized him suddenly
and without mercy.

Now he is tended to
by the priesthood of
the intravenous line.

One arm salt water
chill, from grasping
the Formorian foe.

The other liquid silver,
a magical morphine
rush of warmth.

He is a god restored,
a king made whole.
Then sleep claims him.

And he cannot fight
this beautiful dream,
even if he wanted to.

Crescent

I trimmed my thumbnail
and couldn't find the off-cut.

Many hours later I saw it
hanging in the sky.

Death Is Not a Fate; It Is an End

I read another poet's poem about dying.
It spoke of death like a mother
waiting to gather her in from the garden
where she played in a pretty dress.
She's dead now (she got a prize for it).

The poem spoke of comfort I think.
Everyone said how warm it made them feel.
Another one of hers I saw said
she felt like a pretty flower
whose stem had been cut but
still it bloomed or something.

I have woken up full of fury
that the world thinks
that this is how it will be:
'He died peacefully, surrounded by family and friends.'

Why not: 'He died irritated and in some pain,
after calling a cunt a cunt because he was having
a bad day, not knowing it was his last'?

I read one of her books many years ago.
It was very good. I hope she had a good death.
I would like to have met her, compared notes, had a joke.

The Sea

The deep memory of
the womb and its amniotic
tide is not why it calls us,
soothes us, kills us.

It is because it is the Sea.

THANKS TO:

Lana, not just for her love and support, but for copy-editing and proofreading.

One Darnley Road, creative agency extraordinaire, especially to Rob and Róisín, for their skill, creativity and generosity.

My friends James Arber, Colin Brush and Nick Lake, for their time, help and encouragement.

Harry Man for his early assurance that I wasn't a talentless dabbler.

All who were kind enough to read and react to my work, despite the many more important demands on their time and energy. I really appreciate it.

And to my mum and dad, for a home and a childhood where books were simply a part of life.

B~

Printed in Great Britain
by Amazon

48354150R00037